FAVORITE DESIGNER DOGS

Pebble® Plus

You'll Love

Morkies

by Erin Edison

Gail Saunders-Smith PhD,
Consulting Editor

CAPSTONE PRESS
a capstone imprint

Pebble Plus is published by Capstone Press,
1710 Roe Crest Drive, North Mankato, Minnesota 56003
www.capstonepub.com

Library of Congress Cataloging-in-Publication Data
Edison, Erin, author.
You'll love morkies / Erin Edison.
    pages cm.—(Favorite designer dogs) (Pebble plus)
Summary: "Simple text and full-color photographs describe the characteristics and care of the Morkie, a cross between a Maltese and a Yorkshire terrier."—Provided by publisher.
Includes bibliographical references and index.
ISBN 978-1-4914-0571-0 (hb)—ISBN 978-1-4914-0639-7 (pb)—ISBN 978-1-4914-0605-2 (eb)
1. Morkie—Juvenile literature. 2. Toy dogs—Juvenile literature. 3. Dog breeds—Juvenile literature. I. Title.
SF429.M67E35 2015
636.76—dc23

                                                                                2014001833

Editorial Credits
Erika L. Shores, editor; Kyle Grenz, designer; Katy LaVigne, production specialist

Photo Credits
Alamy: blickwinkel, 11, imagebroker, 9; Capstone Studio: Karon Dubke, cover, 1, 7, 17, 19; Shutterstock: Ali Peterson, 13, Eric Isselee, 5, JStaley401, 15, Sergey Lavrentev, 5; SuperStock: Exactostock, 21

Design Elements
Shutterstock: Julynx

Note to Parents and Teachers

The Favorite Designer Dogs series supports national science standards related to life science. This book describes and illustrates Morkies, a cross between a Maltese and a Yorkshire terrier. The images support early readers in understanding the text. The repetition of words and phrases helps early readers learn new words. This book also introduces early readers to subject-specific vocabulary words, which are defined in the Glossary section. Early readers may need assistance to read some words and to use the Table of Contents, Glossary, Read More, Internet Sites, and Index sections of the book.

Printed in the United States of America in North Mankato, Minnesota.
042014   008087CGF14

Table of Contents

What Is a Morkie?

Little Morkies are designer dogs.

Designer dogs are a mix

of two dog breeds.

The Maltese and the Yorkshire

terrier make up a Morkie.

Maltese

Yorkshire terrier

Morkies can be full of energy.
In this way, they are like
Yorkshire terriers, or Yorkies.
But Morkies also enjoy sitting
on laps like Maltese do.

You might spot Morkies anywhere. They're about the size of a football.

Some owners carry their Morkies in purses.

The Morkie Look

Yorkies and Maltese are small dogs. Morkies are no different. They stand less than 10 inches (25 centimeters) tall.

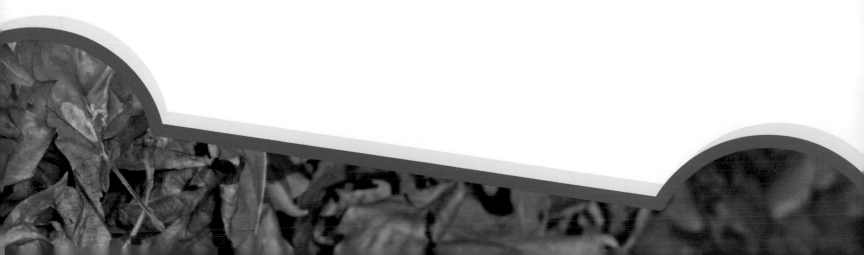

Most Morkies look alike.

But some Morkie ears stick up.

Other Morkie ears hang down.

Coats are brown, white, black,

or a mix of colors.

Puppy Time

A newborn Morkie weighs less than an apple. Adults weigh less than 7 pounds (3 kilograms). With good care, Morkies live up to 14 years.

Caring for Morkies

Morkies eat two to four meals each day. Give them food made for small dogs. It will be the right size for their little mouths.

A Morkie's long coat tangles and gets dirty easily. Bathing and brushing helps a Morkie look and feel good.

Mini Watchdogs

Morkies are loyal pets.
Some Morkies act like
watchdogs. They bark
at strange noises or people.

Glossary

breed—a certain kind of animal within an animal group

coat—an animal's hair or fur

energy—the strength to do active things without getting tired

loyal—being true to someone or something

tangle—to twist together in a clump

Read More

Armentrout, David and Patricia. *Doggie Duties.* Let's Talk About Pets. Vero Beach, Fla.: Rourke Publishing, 2011.

Hart, Joyce. *Small Dogs.* Great Pets. New York: Marshall Cavendish Benchmark, 2009.

Stone, Lynn M. *Maltese.* Eye to Eye with Dogs. Vero Beach, Fla.: Rourke Pub., 2009.

Internet Sites

FactHound offers a safe, fun way to find Internet sites related to this book. All of the sites on FactHound have been researched by our staff.

Here's all you do:

Visit *www.facthound.com*

Type in this code: 9781491405710

Check out projects, games and lots more at
www.capstonekids.com

Index

Word Count: 198
Grade: 1
Early-Intervention Level: 14